This Changes Everything

Dr. Paul Perkins

Copyright

All material in this book is copyrighted and any reproduction of the material, for any reason, is welcomed. Pass it along as many times as you wish.

ISBN-13:

978-1723177774

ISBN-10:

1723177776

Chapter 1
Foundation

Jesus changes everything. However, before we can focus on what that means, I want to lay out some basic and fundamental presuppositions. Presuppositions are the bedrock of our worldview. Our worldview is the lens through which we see and interpret the world. For example:

If your worldview believes that animals have the same rights as humans, you will look at cattle farming differently than a person whose worldview sees animals as a source of protein. One will enjoy a steak and the other will do everything they can to set it free. Worldviews are important to understand.

Therefore, to understand why I believe that Jesus changes everything you need some background to my worldview. Here we go. There are four basic dictums that ground me in my understanding of life, the universe and everything.

1.   God exists and he is personal.
2.   God created humans to live in relationship with him.

3. Humans, through Adam and Eve, rebelled against God and received a just sentence.

4. God went to extreme measures to reestablish his relationship with mankind.

Looking for answers to a meaningful life must start with the question, "Where did we come from?" Philosophers, religionists, and scientists have all pondered this question, and the answers vary depending on your worldview. I have answered the question for myself based on the following:

1. If I have the capacity to think, then humanity was created by a thinking being.

2. If I have a capacity to love/express emotion, then humanity was created by a being with emotion.

3. If I have the capacity for creativity, then humanity was created by a creative being.

4. If I have a capacity for justice then, humanity was created by a just being.

There are many more evidences for God's existence and that express his personal nature. These alone, however, do not

explain all the issues of our world, but it is where it starts. It continues in how the pinnacle of God's creation expresses itself. Having been created in the image of God we learn about God's nature by exploring the virtuous parts of humanities nature.

At the core of humanities nature is the desire to live in relationship. From an atheist's perspective, it's all about hormones and pheromones. Yet, the delicate balance created in men and women is the act of a loving creator who understands relationships. God himself exists in a delicate balance of three persons and one essence. The trinity is the dance between the father, son, and Holy Spirit, where each is distinct, yet, is all that the others is. All this to say that humans are made for relationships.

Humanity has always been drawn together in order to form communities, where every individual contributes, and the collective protects one another. It is in those communities where we learn to love one another and have a relationship with God. In the beginning God was the protector and provider. Humanity and its creator lived in perfect harmony.

I am always amazed when I read the book of Genesis. At the height of God's creative work, in the most intimate moment of the morning garden, he finds out that he was betrayed. Adam and

Eve sinned by disobedience, and the sin was so egregious that it deserved death. If God had taken Adam's life in payment for their sin, it would not haven been sufficient. The rebellious act against God was considered so terrible that a holy God could not allow it to go unpunished, and one human wasn't enough. So, all of creation was cursed until the time God brought about a solution that only he could accomplish.

"For God so loved the world that he sacrificed his own son, that whoever believes in him will have eternal life." John 3:16

"No greater love than this, that a man lay his life down for a friend." John 15:3.

Yet, God goes one step further. He sends his son (Jesus) to die for his enemies (Romans 5:10). It is an unselfish act of grace, mercy, kindness, love, justice, holiness, and service. These are the presumptions that fashion my worldview. They are also the cornerstone by which people can find true meaning and purpose.

If you don't believe these presuppositions, that's alright. As you read through the book, jot down questions that you can ask someone you know, or you can send them to me

(pandrperkins@gmail.com). My only prayer is that you will find the true path. It is narrow, but it is worth the journey.

Chapter 2
My Story

Does Jesus make a difference? I suppose it depends on your relationship with him. We all have stories. Stories of family, stories of faith, even stories of joy and tragedy. In each of these stories lies a deep need to connect with something bigger than ourselves. Here is my story.

My family was typical of the 1950s. Mom and dad, three boys and a dog. My father was a Sargent in the United States Air Force. My mom was a nurse. My dad didn't have any religious affiliation and my mom was raised in a small town Methodist Church. They were products of a religious moral society, at least on the outside. They believed in a God, in family, in their commitment to one another in marriage. They loved us boys as best they could and hoped for the rest.

My father spent most of my childhood stationed oversees, leaving my mom to cope with three rowdy boys. She went through a depression, and unlike today there were no support groups. She

took her frustrations out on my oldest brother. I remember her dragging him by the hair, he hadn't done something right. In return he took his anger out on his two younger brothers, I being the youngest.

There was always this undercurrent of anger in our home. My brothers turned to drugs, my mom to drinking, and I poured myself into materialism. There was strength in possessing what others wished they had. My brothers always came to me for money, and I could trigger their kindness or anger. When it came down to it we were all lonely people looking for something.

As a military child, who moved about every two years, the one thing we longed for and lacked were relationships with our peers. As an adult, military personel were able to form quick bonds and release them as quickly when they left. For me it was another reason to isolate myself. Why make friends if they wouldn't last. And even the friendships I did make were shallow and self fulfilling.

After several confrontations with the law, drugs, and errant children my dad decided to retire. He wanted to spend time with the family, but it was too late. In the end he died from a heart attack, 55 years old and an alcoholic. Years before his death, mom had asked if anyone wanted to go to church with her. It was an

intriguing proposition. I had toyed with mysticism, atheism, and Christianity. *Since she was going*, I thought. *I might as well.*

Over the course of a month we visited a Methodist church, Presbyterian church, and a Southern Baptist Church. They were all the same and reminded me of the military services we seldom attended. It was the Southern Baptist Church where the Youth Pastor came to visit. He was a nice man with a thick southern drawl. He invited me to attend their youth group. I politely said I would think about it.

There was no good reason for me to go. I didn't know anyone. Christian teens at my school were weird. I had a girlfriend and my self-serving lifestyle was doing alright for me. But I went, and the girls were cute and friendly. And it was because of them that I kept going back. There was nothing special about the program. We sat in a circle and Pastor Larry taught out of the Bible. Afterward we would go get ice cream. If I was looking for a church with a lot of pizzazz, that wasn't it.

There was something different about these kids. They genuinely loved each other, and they showed it to me. When I didn't come I got a call. When I did come I was greeted like a prince. In this group I received something that I deeply longed for—real friends. I was starved for authentic relationships. I had a

girlfriend who was already planning our wedding. But our relationship was shallow. It eventually ended.

Then one day it clicked. It was as if scales dropped from my eyes and the darkness that had blinded me was gone. I could see for the first time why my life was shaped like it was. Sin had trashed my family, and I felt on the outside. My life was marked by my sinful attitude and lusts. I needed a savior and the father sent his son. I needed a family and God gave me the church.

I was never a terribly bad individual. Unlike my brothers I didn't do drugs, drink, womanize, and run the tight edge of the law. In fact, when I became a Christian my behavior didn't change that much. What changed was how I saw the world. I understood the root of my family's dysfunction. I knew that it would never change on its own. And I knew if I didn't get out of there I would end up like them.

So, one day I went to brother Larry's office and asked what I needed to do to be saved. From that day on I poured my life into the church. I learned what forgiveness meant, what real love is, how to deal with anger and confess when I when it boiled to the surface. I have been a Jesus follower now for 43 years, married to a wonderful women, three boys who love the Lord, their wives and their children. There have been rough patches, questioning

roads, winding paths, but never have I ever doubted my faith in Jesus. He changed everything for me, and I will always be eternally grateful.

Sounds likes a dream come true, but life is always about the day after "happily ever after." Tragedy tests our faith. Four nephews and one niece all died before they were twenty-five. Drinking and drugs can take a terrible toll on people. They shatter lives and destroy families.

My youngest son developed type 1 diabetes, and that changed our lives. My glorious entrance into the church eroded as I found that people are messy, everyone needs a savior, and that the road to the Kingdom of God is fraught with dangers and pitfalls. As I get older I wrestle with health issues, aches and pains that will be with me for the rest of my life. Yet, through it all Jesus has made all the difference. Hope is powerful. Hope in an all powerful, all loving, all caring God is life changing; life sustaining.

The rest of this book explores what it is about Jesus that makes such a difference in people's lives. Lord willing, in your life.

Chapter 3
Resurrection

Jesus said, "I am the resurrection and the life, he who believes in me, even if he dies, he will live forever" (John 11:25).w

Jesus said this to a young woman whose brother had died three days earlier. Mary and Martha hoped Jesus would make it to their house before their brother died. They knew Jesus would heal him. Now he was dead. She believed Jesus could heal, but raise someone from the dead? That was beyond belief. That's what Jesus loved doing, take a person to the brink of their faith and then amaze them with something more extraordinary.

The Resurrection of Jesus from the dead changed everything! Christians put a lot of faith in the saving power of Jesus' sacrifice, but it was his resurrection that put a stamp of power on the atonement. The Apostle Paul wrote, "If Christ has not been raised, your faith is futile and you are still in your sins,"

12

(1 Corinthians 15:17). It seems so fantastic! But everything hinges on Christ's promise of a resurrection.

History is verified by several factors. What is the archeological evidences? What eyewitness accounts are there and are they credible? What is the written record and is it accurate? I'm not going to go into all the evidence to convince you of the resurrection, but I do want to look at a few that the Apostle Paul lays out for his readers. 1 Corinthians 15:3-8 says,

> For I delivered to you as of first importance what I also received: that Christ died for our sins in accordance with the Scriptures, that he was buried, that he was raised on the third day in accordance with the Scriptures, and that he appeared to Cephas, then to the twelve. Then he appeared to more than five hundred brothers at one time, most of whom are still alive, though some have fallen asleep. Then he appeared to James, then to all the apostles. Last of all, as to one untimely born, he appeared also to me.

Paul is relaying accounts as he had received them from Jesus himself. Paul was a persecutor of the church, and when he had a dramatic experience with the risen Christ he turned from an

enemy of Christ to one of the greatest proponents of the faith. It was a dramatic turn around that changed everything for him.

Yet, Paul doesn't solely lay the claim of Jesus' resurrection on his experience alone. He points back to the scripture. Isaiah 53 is a prophetic description of the suffering of Jesus. In the last verse Jesus' resurrection was prophesied, "and makes intercession for transgressors." He could not make intercession if he were dead. Psalm 16:10 also says that God would not allow Jesus to languish in Sheol. The scripture declared it, therefore, we can be certain of it. Yet, knowing our lack of faith God provided eyewitness accounts.

He first appeared to Cepheus, who is also called Peter. After that he showed himself to the 12 apostles. The big one is that he appeared to over 500 people at one time. And if Paul's readers wanted to verify the facts, many of those people were still alive. He then appeared to James, his brother. Jesus' family didn't believe in him until after the resurrection. They saw his life as a waste, and his death a tragedy. But after his resurrection James was transformed and even died a martyr for the faith.

I know the arguments against these accounts. I agree that faith in the Bible as God's word and that what Paul says is true is necessary. Yet, history bears out the testimony, the transformed

lives, the willingness to live and die for someone they knew to have died and rise from the grave. You see the resurrection changes everything.

Why is the resurrection so important?

- Hope for our own resurrection
- Confidence in the power of Jesus' death over sin
- Perseverance in the face of persecution knowing that this life is just a short part of our journey
- Contentment in the blessings God has given us because our store house of riches is in the kingdom
- Power over the evil one who could not conquer Jesus through death.
- Jesus' return in power to establish his kingdom once and for all

Paul said, "Death is swallowed up in victory." "O death, where is your victory?

O death, where is your sting?" The sting of death is sin, and the power of sin is the law. But thanks, be to God, who gives us the victory through our Lord Jesus Christ.

1 Corinthians 15:55-57.

Our culture puts a premium on youth. We spend billions of dollars on health foods, cosmetics, medical procedures, all for the purpose of staying young. Why? Because death scares us. But there is no fear in that which we have conquered. It's like the bully on the playground. No one wants to cross him for fear that he would pick on them. But when he is finally vanquished, by a peer or an adult, there is rejoicing. Fear chains us, victory frees us.

Yes, we will all probably die. But when our eyes close in this life and open in the glorious presence of God we will finally understand. The resurrection changes everything!

Chapter 4
Servant

Jesus said, "Even the son of man did not come into the world to be served, but to serve and to give my life as a ransom for many" (Mark 10:45).

 I read once that in a struggling economy restaurants can still thrive. People like to be served. There is something special about pulling up to a restaurant and having someone open your car door. That's why America's economy is called a "service" economy. When I shop on eBay the most sought after product is the customer review, not any review, but 4 and 5 star reviews. Bad costumer service reviews will end up losing a company money.

 Even Jesus' disciples were part of the 'serve' culture of their time. They were walking along talking, loud enough for Jesus to hear, and they were arguing about who would be the greatest. Jesus said,

  The kings of the Gentiles exercise lordship over them, and those in authority over them are called benefactors. But not

so with you. Rather, let the greatest among you become as the youngest, and the leader as one who serves. Luke 22:25,26.

The world exercises lordship, they like to boss people around. It starts young. Put children in a room with toys and eventually one will rise to the top and start bossing the others. If two rise to the top someone gets bit. A friend of mine always said, "it's not how big the dog is, but how big the bite." That's the way of the world, but Jesus requires something different.

He came to serve. All throughout the gospels Jesus traveled around healing and preaching. He comforted, had compassion, touched the untouchable, and spoke to the lonely. His was a heart of service. But Jesus wasn't a doormat. He had boundaries, especially for those who only wanted to kill him. In fact Jesus told the people they couldn't serve two masters. They had to make choices and alliances. Service is crucial, but who you serve is even more important.

Then the righteous will answer him, saying, 'Lord, when did we see you hungry and feed you, or thirsty and give you drink? And when did we see you a stranger and

18

welcome you, or naked and clothe you? And when did we see you sick or in prison and visit you?' And the King will answer them, Truly, I say to you, as you did it to one of the least of these my brothers, you did it to me. Matthew 25:37-39.

The rich don't need our help, but the poor, downtrodden, unjustly treated, orphans, and widows need us everyday. When we turn our hearts and efforts toward them we are essentially doing it for Jesus. But why? Why is it so important that Jesus is a servant? How does it change everything?

Jesus didn't come to be served, but to serve AND GIVE HIS LIFE AS A RANSOM FOR SIN! Jesus served in a variety of capacities, but none so great as his death on the cross.

Have this mind among yourselves, which is yours in Christ Jesus, who, though he was in the form of God, did not count equality with God a thing to be grasped, but emptied himself, by taking the form of a servant, being born in the likeness of men. And being found in human form, he humbled himself by becoming obedient to the point of death, even death on a cross. Philippians 2:5-8.

It was the purpose of the Father to send his son to pay the penalty of man's sin. But if God had been as base as humanity he would have clutched his power and let the world be damned. His heart, however, has always been recklessly in love with his creation. Taking off his royal garments, he put on the soiled garments of a servant. But his service wasn't just the groveling acts of peasantry, no, it was the sacrificial death of a king, who was the only one equipped to do what he did. It was the single most selfless act of service any one person could perform!

Some would say that Jesus was merely an example of love and service, not some divine being. That if we follow him we can have the same impact, but that is only partially true. We are to emulate his character and good works, but we could never serve in the capacity of his redeeming love. Only a loving Heavenly Father could plan such an extraordinary act of service.

Christians were among the first to establish hospitals, asylums, work houses for the poor, charities, and schools. Not all turned out to be the altruistic endeavors that is representative of Jesus, but their initial intent was from a sacrificial heart of service.

For you were called to freedom, brothers. Only do not use your freedom as an opportunity for the flesh, but through love serve one another. For the whole law is fulfilled in one word: "You shall love your neighbor as yourself. Galatians 5:13,14.

Service isn't something you do in isolation. It is a community act. We live in communities, we work in communities, and in Christ we live within a community of faith. Jesus said that the world would know we are his disciples if we have love for one another. We can only accomplish this in the context of the family of God. It's a community of another world and when it is lived out the way it is suppose to, it is incredible.

Does Jesus make a difference? You bet he does. He has led the way for countless men, women, and children to set aside their selfish desires for the sake of serving others. Instead of careers where they are financially secure, they have taken vows of poverty to work among the worlds poorest of poor. His example of service isn't enough, though. It is the type of service that changes everything. He gave his life as a ransom for many. He bore a cross so we wouldn't have to, he took on God's wrath in our

21

place, he suffered excruciating pain as a silent servant, that we might stand free from condemnation.

Jesus changes everything!

Chapter 5

Way-Truth-Life

Jesus said, "I am the way, the truth, and the life. No one comes to the father accept through me" (John 14:6).

Have you ever lost your way? It's frightening. In the seventh grade our family lived on the island of Crete. My dad was stationed at an Air Force base. Before being assigned housing, we lived in the Astoria Hotel downtown. I stayed late at school, and had to take the bus from the base to downtown. It stopped right in front of the hotel.

I was sure my parents said they were going to be playing cards at a friend's house. I was also sure I knew which bus stop they lived off of. Neither were true. The sun had gone down and the scattered street lights cast shadows down long and lonely streets. Dogs howled in the distance, some growled close by, and I quickened my pace to…I didn't know. I just kept walking hoping to find my way around the dark and foreboding streets. I was scared and I cried, and sang, and talked to myself. Losing your way in a foreign country was terrifying.

When I thought all was lost, a taxi driver was passing by and stopped and asked if I needed a ride. I obviously was out of place at that time of night. I took him up on his offer only to find that the hotel was just up the hill and around the corner. He went up stairs and my dad paid him. I was never so glad to be home than at that moment.

Jesus said, "Wide is the way that leads to destruction and many find it. Narrow is the way that leads to life and few find it" (Matthew 7:13).

It is easy to lose your way in this life. In fact, we start off on the wrong road. We would continue in the darkness if it weren't for God sending his son. In the book of John, it says, "and the light shone in the darkness, but the darkness did not comprehend it." Just because there is light doesn't mean we will follow the correct path. The only way to heaven is through Jesus. He stands as a door, a gate, a way to the heavenly city, and if we are willing to follow him we will find all the blessings the Father must bestow.

There are ancient paths that are good. If we are discerning they will lead us to understand who Jesus is. But there are also new paths that have been worn by the feet of those who have gone before us. We look to the ancient paths because they anchor us to

our past, but we walk on the new path because it is the way of Jesus

Not only is Jesus the way, but he is also the truth. What is Truth, the philosopher will say? What is Truth, the scientist will argue? What is Truth the religionists will pontificate? What is Truth, Pilot asked Jesus? Jesus didn't answer the question for two reasons. First, there is no arguing someone into the kingdom. Often times people will make a statement like Pilot's as an academic exercise. They are less concerned about the validity as they are about the tactic to win the debate. Secondly, Jesus had already performed enough miracles to validate his claim to truth.

Sincere truth seekers, understand the difficulty of discerning different truth claims. Yet, they are genuinely open to hear someone else and find out where their understanding of truth originates. To start on a quest for truth a person needs a good definition. "That which is true or in accordance with fact or reality" (online dictionary). If this is a correct definition, then the one who has created all things and holds it together should have a greater understanding about the nature of reality and the facts to which it pertains.

He is the image of the invisible God, the firstborn of all creation. For by him all things were created, in heaven and on earth, visible and invisible, whether thrones or dominions or rulers or authorities—all things were created through him and for him. And he is before all things, and in him all things hold together. (Colossians 1:15-17)

Jesus is the only one where reality and facts perfectly meet. In him we see the world for what it is really like. In him we know the true nature of man's soul and its cure. In him the quantum and macro find their connection. Jesus doesn't just show us the truth. Nor does he tell us about the truth. Jesus is the Truth, manifested before our eyes and every other religious scheme, philosophical position, or scientific theorist fears him, and speaks out against him.

Jesus is also the life. The miracle of birth is remarkable. A sperm and egg meet and the next thing you know a baby is developing, growing, and being welcomed into the world. Yet, neither father nor mother can cause it to grow. Humans have no intrinsic force within them that they can control in order to produce life. Only God can cause something to grow. And only Jesus has the intrinsic quality of growth within himself. He is life.

He doesn't become alive. Therefore, whatever he touches has the potential to gain life or lose it. He gives it or he takes it away.

This is why Jesus changes everything. If life resides in Jesus. If death cannot hold him. If he offers new life, abundant life, and eternal life then we can trust that it will come to pass. The old song goes like this:

Because he lives, I can face tomorrow.
Because he lives, all fear is gone.
Because I know he holds the future
Life is worth the living
Just because he lives.

Jesus doesn't just live — he is the author of life.

Jesus is the way, the truth and the life. Why is this important? Because it is the reason we can go through him to get to the Father. No other person on earth, past, present, or future will be able to make this claim and fulfill it. If God has gone to extraordinary lengths to bring us back to him, then to know the way, the truth and the life is a gift worth receiving. If God is so recklessly in love with his creation, then to know the Way, the Truth, and the Life opens us up to experience a limitless and

boundless love. If God was willing to set aside his robe for tattered rags of a servant, then knowing the Way, Truth, and the Life opens up for us extraordinary opportunities to serve others. Through Jesus our renewed relationship with the Father has a depth that only comes through his revelation to us — he IS The Way, The Truth, and The Life.

I'm telling you, Jesus changes everything!

Chapter 6
Light

Jesus said, "I am the light of the world. Whoever follows me will not walk in darkness, but will have the light of life" (John 8:12).

Crawling on our bellies, we inched our way deep into the mountain. Someone said this was fun, but all I remember is scraped knees, dirt in my eyes, and absolute darkness. The lights on our helmet lit the way well enough, but if they went out there was nothing. To emphasize the fact, our guide told everyone to turn off our head lamps. It was eerie and frightening. No light, no sound, and the heavy weight of the earth on top of us. I was ready to get out, back to the glorious light.

Darkness has always been associated with evil, horror, and depravity. Jesus said, "people loved the darkness rather than the light because their works were evil." Sitting around campfires we tell ghost stories. On Halloween, we dress our children up as specters and tell them to yell trick or treat. We have even changed our words. Replacing good words with negative words. Instead of good we say, that's bad. Or we call something we like "bitchin".

Seemingly innocuous activities seep into our culture until we can't tell the difference between right or wrong.

The gospel of John paints a picture in its first chapter. The world has become darkened because of sin. The Father is sending his son (the true light) into the world to bring truth and grace. This is how John described it.

> The true light, which gives light to everyone, was coming into the world. He was in the world, and the world was made through him, yet the world did not know him. He came to his own, and his own people did not receive him. (John 1:9-11)

How frustrating it must have been. Jesus had created the world. It was his and it lay in darkness. The Father sends him, Immanuel, God is with us, and yet the world did not recognize him. But, how could it? Darkness obscures, it casts shadows, it creates monsters where there is none. On top of that the prince of darkness blinds the world from the light. How in all of creation is Jesus going to change things?

The nature of light and darkness gives us a hint. Darkness isn't anything, rather it is the absence of light. It is empty,

powerless, and meaningless against true light. Jesus is the true light who came into the world, and though he was not recognized the darkness had to flee. In absolute darkness light is welcomed, but in shades of gray we get use to the little light we have and become comfortable.

Because we are created in the image of God there is enough light to make us feel good about our good works. We aren't so bad, look at how bad those people are without any light. At least I have some. Surely God will take that into account? But our gray world corrupts even the little amount of goodness we can muster until in the end it too is darkness.

While in our darkness Jesus comes, and with his light he brings life. Darkness obscures what true life's all about. In my home growing up yelling was a typical way of engaging differences. The loudest person wins. In my wife's home (all were Christians) no one raised their voices at each other. After we were married we had our first real fight. I yelled and she cried. I couldn't figure out why she was crying. Fight back, that's what I wanted.

Growing up in darkness I assumed that our conflict resolution style was normal and good. We didn't pull knives on each other, but the intent was still the same; overcome through

power. With my wife, I experienced a new and better way. It wasn't easy to change my habits, but her gentleness made me want to. When exposed to light, darkness flees. When exposed to light not even the shadows can remain, but it doesn't happen instantly. The god of this world does not let go easily.

> In their case the god of this world has blinded the minds of the unbelievers, to keep them from seeing the light of the gospel of the glory of Christ, who is the image of God. (2 Corinthians 4:4).

How does that happen? How can people miss the simplicity of the good news? Because deception touches the blind with just enough truth that keeps them off balance. It goes like this:

> "Hey, John I've been watching your work over the past few months, and it is extraordinary. You have a great work ethic. What is it that drives you to do your best every day."

> "Thank you, Mr. Carson for the kind words. If I can be open, I would say it is my relationship with Jesus. Because

of what he has done on the cross, I feel compelled, with a full heart of gratitude to do my best in all circumstances. Do you go to church anywhere, Mr. Carson?"

Well, uhh, no. I used to, but it wasn't for me, too many hypocrites. You know what I mean? People who do one thing on Sunday and then do another during the week. I just wanted to say thank you for your hard work."

Are there hypocrites in the church? Sure. Are their sinners in the church? You're looking at one. It is this truth that Satan uses to keep people away from the light. They know something is different, they know that they want something more, but they are afraid to lose themselves to the light.

Darkness also promises what it can't deliver. Christians should be careful not to fall into the trap of offering what is not in their power to grant. "Turn to Jesus and everything will be all right." "Give money to the church and you will receive it back tenfold."

A missionary sat with a young mother whose child had a debilitating deformity. The missionary was sharing the

gospel when the woman asked, "will Jesus heal my daughter?"

The missionary responded, "Jesus can heal your daughter, but he doesn't promise that he will. We can only pray."

The mother pondered the statement for a little while then answered, "I will continue to worship the sea goddess. She promises to heal my son."

The good news is that when we choose to follow Jesus his light shines in the darkness, and we become bearers of the light to a dark world.

You are the light of the world. A city set on a hill cannot be hidden. Nor do people light a lamp and put it under a basket, but on a stand, and it gives light to all in the house. In the same way, let your light shine before others, so that they may see your good works and give glory to your Father who is in heaven. (Matthew 5:14-16).

Just as Jesus shines in the darkness so do we. We can't hide it, even if we try. It is not ours to keep. As Christians we are called be ready, in season and out of season, to give an answer for the hope that resides in us. Can you see it now? Can you see how Jesus changes everything?

Chapter 7
Sheep Door

Jesus said, "I am the door of the sheep. All who came before me are thieves and robbers, but the sheep did not listen to them. I am the door. If anyone enters by me, he will be saved and will go in and out and find pasture" (John 10:7-9).

Doors can be fascinating, especially if you are in a culture where doors are the primary way to decorate the outside of your home. I was in the Middle East walking through the old souk. Souks were the hub of daily life. They were market places and homes. During the day, when life was much slower in the heat, you could take your time and wander the streets looking at doors.

These doors ranged from blues, to reds, to bronze and burnt out. They were not just beautiful carvings, but behind them were stories of people, their lives and their loves. These doors represented mystery and intrigue. Secrets lay within; all this lay behind the door, just beyond your imagination.

Doors can either be invitations or barriers to relationships. When you walk up to a house, one of the first things you are

greeted to is the door. Have you ever thought about how that door made you feel? Was it all wood or metal? Was it plain or painted? Was it solid or were there windows? I like doors that have windows. They feel more inviting, as if to say there are no secrets behind these doors. My least favorite door is a solid wooden door with an iron gate in front of it. It makes me feel as if I entered, I would never come out.

That's the door themselves, but what about the people who come to your door? Do they see you look through the peep hole, or is there a camera to assessing the guest before engaging them? Strangers outside your door can create fear and apprehension. Are they wearing uniforms? What kind of uniforms, military or business? Do they look clean cut or disheveled? Our society has made us weary of strangers and we take extreme measures to protect ourselves behind our doors. Living in the darkness has made us suspicious of anyone on the other side of the door. Too many stories of thieves breaking in and destroying.

On the other hand, when someone you love, someone who has been gone for a long time, comes to the door, you grin from ear to ear and the greeting is warm and lively. Familiar faces break down barriers, create a feeling of warmth, and security. With friends, we often stand with the door open because the

conversation continues, even when they said they needed to go. Welcoming doors have lights and mats and pretty knockers. Welcoming doors see strangers as opportunities to be hospitable.

> Do not neglect to show hospitality to strangers, for thereby some have entertained angels unawares. Hebrews 13:2.

Jesus describes himself as a shepherd, and he has specific sheep who hang out with him. They come in and out as they please. They are his sheep and they know him as the faithful door. They see him and know he won't harm them. They enter through him and know they will be safe. They go back through and are not afraid that he will abandon them.

But he wasn't the only one who claimed to be a door. There were those who came before him, who only wanted to do harm to the community. They were wolves in sheep clothing, and desired to rob and destroy the shepherd's sheep. They were open doors, but their welcome brought death. Sometimes they were pretty doors, and their alluringly glittering structure tempted lustful eyes. Others were strong doors, but when they closed behind you it was a trap.

38

Only the shepherd's door brings life, but it is important to know his name, his voice, and his call. That comes from spending time with him, listening for his voice, and heeding his call. We are blessed to have the Word of God to read, memorize, and study so that we are able to discern the voice of the shepherd and enter by the true door.

When I was young our family watched the TV game show "Let's Make a Deal." At some point in the show there were always three doors, and behind one of the doors was a fabulous prize. Everyone in the audience shouted which door the contestant should pick until the frenzy was at such a pitch that they finally gave an answer. The anticipation kept us at the edge of our seats, and then they went to a commercial.

For us it is different. The doors are open, some are filled with riches, some with temptations of the flesh, others offer fame and fortune and power. The Door of the sheep stands open and calls out names, familiar names, names just like me, my name. The glitter and glamour of the other doors fade compared to the glory and love of the shepherd's door. Waking from the slumber of death, there is a flood of peace and joy. Before me is a banquet table full of friends and family.

Jesus changes everything!

Chapter 8
Abundant Life

Jesus said, "I have come to give you life and to give it abundantly" (John 10:10).

Webster online dictionary defines life this way:

- the quality that distinguishes a vital and functional being from a dead body
- a principle or force that is considered to underlie the distinctive quality of animate beings
- an organismic state characterized by capacity for metabolism, growth, reaction to stimuli, and reproduction
- the sequence of physical and mental experiences that make up the existence of an individual

Notice the variety of adjectives: qualities, vital, functioning, principle or force, distinctive quality, organismic state, and physical and mental experiences. Life can not be defined in a simple sentence. We are beautifully created, each part fine tuned with purpose. Of course, the curse of original sin has

marred what God had meant to be wonderful. Yet, even amid sin's damage our humanness is uniquely remarkable.

Jesus came to give us life, but what kind of life is he promising? What will be different for me by following Jesus? The word life can be used in a variety of ways, and is defined by its context. Jesus came to give eternal life. That is an after-death promise.

Jesus came to give us life, a new way of living, a kingdom way of life. This type of life involves rules, laws, and community. When Jesus preached that the kingdom of God was at hand he was offering people a new way of living.

Jesus came to give us life, as a quality of being, contentment, peace, and security. It's the type of life that no matter what the circumstances, there is always hope in Christ. Though Jesus came to bring us eternal and kingdom life, I believe his statement of abundance applies to the quality of life, and he promises to deliver it in abundance.

There are three things that are important to know when we talk about a quality life. It involves growth, change and reproduction. Without these qualities, there is no life, and Jesus said he wants to give us this kind of life in abundance.

When my first son was born, it was a marvelous experience. He was tiny as he lay quietly in his mother's arms. She was tired, but the smile on her face as she looked into the eyes of that little baby said it all. But he didn't stay little very long. We were constantly buying, borrowing, and trading clothes to fit his ever-changing body. It never seemed to stop. Though it was gradual, he seemed to pop up over night.

We loved it when he turned over, marveled when he crawled, laughed when he first walked, and was petrified when he started to drive. He grew in knowledge and stature. It is the nature of living things to grow. So when Jesus said he came to give us life he meant for us to grow.

"Like newborn infants, long for the pure spiritual milk," 1 Peter 2:2.

Like newborns we are to hunger for spiritual milk. That is we should hunger for the Bible, want to pray, and be with others in worship. But if we stay here, suckling the goodness of milk, we will miss out on the abundance Jesus promised.

For though by this time you ought to be teachers, you need someone to teach you again the basic principles of the oracles of God. You need milk, not solid food, for everyone who lives on milk is unskilled in the word of righteousness, since he is a child. But solid food is for the mature, for those who have their powers of discernment trained by constant practice to distinguish good from evil. (Hebrew 5:12-14)

Maturity is applying what you have learned. If a person stays in Bible studies all the time and never puts the scripture into practice he is still an infant. What does it look like when a baby Christian grows? First he devours the word of God. Then he has a desire to be in God's presence in prayer and worship. The next step in growth is to be in relationship with other believers, holding each other accountable for life. It is in this context he develops his spiritual gifts, and applies them in service. At this stage, he is doing.

As he grows he not only serves, but he grows in his moral ethic. Change is necessary for growth, not just outward change but inward change. The Holy Spirit resides in the believer to strengthen his powers of discernment, his ability to forgive, to do

good to his enemies, and bless his persecutors. Without this kind of change the believer gets stuck in adolescence, with a consumer mindset, always looking for someone else to do the work.

The final stage of living things is reproduction. Someone might ask, "isn't death the final stage?" Good question. In the insect world reproduction often brings about death. Especially for the male. In larger mammals, they continue reproduction until they no longer are viable. Often the alpha is challenged. If he is too old and loses he will eventually die.

Every living creature is driven to reproduce, only humans choose not to. As followers of Jesus we are called to reproduce spiritually, to serve and pass on what we know about Jesus, this is called discipleship. Discipleship is the process of taking a new believer and growing him to maturity, which means he can reproduce what he has learned in the life of others.

But we were never meant to stay an infant. Growing is a necessity. Look at any plant, if it doesn't grow then it eventually dies. For you to reproduce you need to be in a group of people who will help you learn to serve and to reach out to others. Then you need to find someone to pour your life into for a year or two, so that they can grow and then reproduce.

As we grow we learn to trust and depend on Jesus more and more every day. Some of the lessons revolve around relationships. How do I love more deeply? How do I forgive more readily? How do I communicate clearly? How do I learn to let go of what is not important?

Some lessons center on finances. How do I learn to be content with what God has blessed me with? How do I learn to be more giving to the church, to the less fortunate, to missions? How do I order my finances so I have no debt?

Some lessons are about your relationship with God. What does it mean to abide in the Spirit? How do I approach God with confidence yet, with deep respect and awe? How to I repent when I have sinned and be set free from its guilt? How do I have a deep peace that can only come from God?

Other lessons look outward to the world. How do I reach out without being stained by its sin? How do I share my story so that others will understand the gospel? How do I live in the world without being a part of it?

When we learn, these lessons the follower of Jesus will experience the abundant life God has offered through His son. Then we will discover what it truly means, "Jesus changes everything."

Chapter 9
Living Water

Jesus said, "If anyone thirsts, let him come to me and drink. Whoever believes in me, as the Scripture has said, "Out of his heart will flow rivers of living water" John 7:37,38.

Water. We take it for granted. We use it to water our lawns, wash our clothes and brush our teeth. We bath in it and drink it. It is as essential as air, and without it we die. In the animal kingdom, it brings them together, but in the kingdom of man it may one day be the cause of world conflict. It embodies deep and rich symbolism within world cultures, and in the Bible, it points people to the true source of life, Jesus. Here are some observations from the Bible:

- Water was the cause of destruction— Noah
- Water was a barrier between life and death — the Red Sea
- Water came from a rock — sustaining life in the desert
- Water impeded the conquest of Israel's home — Jordan River

- Water was used in Jesus' first miracle — turned water to wine
- Water drowned the pigs — overcoming Satan
- Water was walked on by Jesus and Peter —revealing the nature of Christ and man
- Water is the new circumcision — Identifying new believers
- Water fills the river of life — coming from the throne of God.

In the classic story Jesus meets a woman at a well. She doesn't know him. She doesn't even know herself. There was something missing she had tried to fill herself, but she was lost. Deep down she longed for someone to show her the way, but a life of men with no real relationships had left her scarred. Shunned from the women in her village, she scraped by, surviving the only way she knew how.

"Give me some water," Jesus said.

His stature was different, soft, not condemning. He looked like a Jewish rabbi, but he didn't judge her, he just asked for water. "Why do you ask me, a Samaritan woman for water?" Years of being ostracized left her suspicious of men who asked for

anything. They only wanted one thing from her. Yet, this Jewish man, who even under normal situations wouldn't have anything to do with a Samaritan has spoken to her.

Jesus answered her, "If you knew the gift of God, and who it is that is saying to you, 'Give me a drink,' you would have asked him, and he would have given you living water."

The woman didn't grasp the deeper meaning of Jesus statement. Physical water is all she knew, and even that was a tiresome chore. "The woman said to him, "Sir, give me this water, so that I will not be thirsty or have to come here to draw water." Physical needs often obscure our ability to discern deep spiritual matter.

Jesus, however, was more concerned with moral issues, "You are right in saying, 'I have no husband'; for you have had five husbands, and the one you now have is not your husband. What you have said is true." She was an adulterous woman, deserving of stoning. The woman quickly changed the topic. But Jesus masterfully guided her back to the topic at hand; that only the Spirit of God, who indwells all who believe, can bring about the spring of living water, refreshing to the soul, life of the spirit.

The disciples approached and reproached Jesus for talking to a Samaritan woman. But she went back to her village, full of

life giving water, and invited all the towns people to come and see such an extraordinary man. The disciples were like the woman; blinded by the world's thinking. Us and them, their's and ours, the world is locked in segregation, competition, and litigation. Worried that they would be contaminated, the disciples would miss an opportunity to love on a stranger. Everyone wants to feel a sense of worth. Jesus Christ makes that happen.

One summer I took ten teens back packing into the Grand Canyon. I was expecting it to be hot, just not 115 degrees. I thought I drank enough water, but I didn't, and in end I suffered heat exhaustion. All I needed to do was drink water. I asked one of the boys (an athlete) how he made it to the top without any difficulties. He said he drank water until it hurt and the drank some more. Life giving water.

Spiritually we think we are filled enough. We read our bibles, go to church, give our money and are content with our spiritual lives; we are filled. But God wants more for us. He wants us to live a life overflowing with possibilities. Jesus called it the abundant life. It comes when our walk in the Spirit spurs us on to love and good deeds; when our love for God and others naturally flows from our lips and our lives.

The filling of the Holy Spirit isn't about running around tents and speaking in a strange language. It is about the power of God flowing through us, to live holy lives before God and to reach out to others with the same love and forgiveness we have received from Christ.

> And this is the testimony, that God gave us eternal life, and this life is in his Son. Whoever has the Son has life; whoever does not have the Son of God does not have life. 1 John 5:11,12.

"This life is in His Son." Living water: refreshing, cleansing, cooling, and life giving. Living Water: gracious, forgiving, merciful, and loving. These are the characteristics of the indwelling Spirit. Displaying spiritual characteristics doesn't guarantee the Spirit, but having the Spirit guarantees their potential. It is our responsibility, through faith, to live out the abundant life we have been given.

Living waters. No one likes hot, stale water. No one likes a hot stale Christian either. Dive in, enjoy the living, flowing waters of life. That's what Jesus gives. That's how Jesus changes everything.

For the Lamb amid the throne will be their shepherd, and he will guide them to springs of living water, and God will wipe away every tear from their eyes (Revelation 7:17).

Chapter 10
Good Shepherd

Jesus said, "I am the good shepherd. I know my own and my own know me, just as the Father knows me and I know the Father; and I lay down my life for the sheep" (John 10:14,15).

The following is taken from Manners and Customs of the Bible by Fred H. Wright, 1953

Food planned for the flock. One of the principal duties at all seasons of the year is for the shepherd to plan food for his flock. In the springtime, there is an abundance of green pasture, and usually the sheep are allowed to graze near to the village where the shepherd's home is located. After the grain is reaped, and the poor have had an opportunity to glean what is left for them, then the shepherd brings in his flock, and the sheep feed on certain fresh growths, or dried blades, or an occasional ear of grain that the reapers may have left, or was overlooked by the gleaners. When this source of food is exhausted then the pasture is sought in

other places. The wilderness of Judea which is located along the western side of the Jordan Valley is carpeted in the spring with a certain amount of grass and this turns into standing hay as the hot weather comes, and this becomes food for the sheep during part of the summer.

Water provided for the flock. In selecting pasturage for the flock, it is an absolute necessity that water be provided, and that it be easy of access. Often flocks are stationed near to a stream of running water. But the sheep are apt to be afraid of drinking water that moves quickly, or that is agitated. Therefore, the shepherd looks for pools of water, or provides some quiet place where they may quench their thirst. How appropriate then are the words concerning the divine Shepherd: "He leadeth me beside the still waters" (Psalm 23:2). But when all such watering places are dried up in the heat of summer, as is often the case in Palestine, then wells are used. Usually a large rock is placed over the mouth of the well and this must be removed, as Jacob did, before the sheep can be watered (Genesis 29:8-10). Noontide is usually the time for watering the sheep. When Jacob was at the well, he said, "Lo, it is yet high day . . .

water ye the sheep" (Genesis 29:7) The matter of water supply plays an important part in locating the flock for pasturage.

Ability to separate the sheep. When it becomes necessary to separate several flocks of sheep, one shepherd after another will stand up and call out: "Tahhoo! Tahhoo!" or a similar call of his own choosing. The sheep lift their heads, and after a general scramble, begin following each one his own shepherd. They are thoroughly familiar with their own shepherd's tone of voice. Strangers have often used the same call, but their attempts to get the sheep to follow them always fail.

Gathering scattered sheep. The shepherd knows how to gather sheep that have been scattered. Especially is this necessary when the sheep must be led back to the fold, or when they are to be guided to another pasture. It is accomplished by his standing in the center of his scattered sheep, and giving them the call which serves as the notes of a bugle do to an army of men. Pebbles are sent by means of his slingshot in the direction of and beyond

members of the flock that fail to heed the call, in order to get their attention and then bring them back. He does not commence to lead them away until he knows they are all there.

The skill of the shepherd, and personal relationship to them is clearly seen when he guides his sheep along narrow paths. The Shepherd Psalm says: "He leadeth me in the paths of righteousness" (Psalm 23:3). The grain fields are seldom fenced or hedged in Bible lands, and sometimes only a narrow path runs between the pasture and these fields. The sheep are forbidden to eat in the fields where crops are growing. Thus, in guiding the sheep along such a path, the shepherd must not allow any of the animals to get into the forbidden area, because if he does, he must pay damages to the owner of the grain. One Syrian shepherd has been known to guide a flock of one hundred fifty sheep without any help, along such a narrow path for quite a distance, without letting a single sheep go where he was not allowed to go.

Intimate knowledge of the sheep. The shepherd is deeply interested in every single one of his flock. Some of them may be given pet names because of incidents connected with them. They are usually counted each evening as they enter the fold, but sometimes the shepherd dispenses with the counting, for he is able to feel the absence of anyone of his sheep. With one sheep gone, something is felt to be missing from the appearance of the entire flock. One shepherd in the Lebanon district was asked if he always counted his sheep each evening. He replied in the negative, and then was asked how then he knew if all his sheep were present. This was his reply: "Master, if you were to put a cloth over my eyes, and bring me any sheep and only let me put my hands on its face, I could tell in a moment if it was mine or not."

Jesus is our good shepherd. He takes care of his own, and we know his voice. So, when we cry out to him he knows our name, and we hear his voice it comforts us in our struggles. There is no greater joy for followers of Jesus than to know that he will guide, protect, and deliver us into the father's arms. That is a good shepherd.

Chapter 11
Not Alone

Jesus said, "I will be with you even until the end of the age" (Matthew 28:20).

When I read Jesus' statement my first thought was "then what?" What happens after the end of the age, but as interesting as it is that's another discussion? To delve into it would take us far astray from our question, "does Jesus make a difference."

The second question that came to my mind was, "why was Jesus giving his disciples this promise?"

All authority in heaven and on earth has been given to me. Go therefore and make disciples of all nations, baptizing them in the name of the Father and of the Son and of the Holy Spirit, teaching them to observe all that I have commanded you. And behold, I am with you always, to the end of the age. Matthew 28:18-29.

57

This is called the everyday commission. It was Jesus' final instruction to his disciples. They were to go out, find faithful men, and reproduce themselves. I would assume that the disciples were apprehensive. The ordeal of the cross, having lost Jesus once was probably weighing on their minds. He was asking a lot of them and then he was going to go; even secretive about his destination.

Maybe that's why he made his exit so dramatic. Seeing him ascend into heaven would have reminded them of his power and glory. And it was that same power that he wanted to give them. What did Jesus tell the disciples?

But you will receive power when the Holy Spirit has come upon you, and you will be my witnesses in Jerusalem and in all Judea and Samaria, and to the end of the earth. Acts 1:8.

I would have been confused, and I think they were too. They went to the upper room in Jerusalem and waited and prayed. They ate and they prayed. They talked about Jesus and all that he said, and they prayed. Then it happened:

And suddenly there came from heaven a sound like a mighty rushing wind, and it filled the entire house where they were sitting. And divided tongues as of fire appeared to them and rested on each one of them. And they were all filled with the Holy Spirit and began to speak in other tongues as the Spirit gave them utterance. Acts 2:2-4.

The Holy Spirit that Jesus promised, came on them in such a mighty and dramatic way that they were compelled into the streets. They spoke in the languages of the visitors to Passover. They spoke of Jesus, and whatever fear they had disappeared in that mighty rushing wind.

The filling of the Holy Spirit is a promise to all new believers, when you place your faith in Jesus as your savior from sin, as the Lord of your life. How does it feel to be filled? Do Christians run around in the streets? How does the Holy Spirit affect our lives?

The Apostle Paul tells us that the Holy Spirit is the seal of our salvation; our stamp of approval. But that isn't all the Holy Spirit does. He guides us, gives insight, convicts of sin, he abides in us, and he leads us into all truth. If Jesus had remained with the disciples physically he would only be in one place at a time. But

the Holy Spirit is able to indwell each believer at the same time. Now that is mind blowing.

As meaningful as it is to be filled with the Spirit, the gift is useless if we are not walking with him. "But I say, walk by the Spirit, and you will not gratify the desires of the flesh" Gal. 5:16. Walking in the Spirit is a continual action, motion in step with another person. Walking in the Spirit takes initiative, concentration, and persistence. But it is the only way we can live as Jesus taught us. You see, the Holy Spirit gives us the ability to put to death desires of the flesh.

Another way of understanding our relationship with the Holy Spirit is, "By this we know that we abide in him and he in us, because he has given us of his Spirit" 1 John 4:13. When we abide we are dwelling in a place with another person. Abiding has the sense of rest from the cares of the world. Abiding is being in the same house and experiencing contentment with another person without the need to talk.

When we abide this way with the Holy Spirit there is an ease with which we learn to trust in his promises. Doubt drifts away and faith burns brighter. No longer does the world loom larger than life, because the life in the Holy Spirit is greater than the world. Abiding in the Holy Spirit allows the believer to see the

world in a completely different way. Instead of fear, there is confidence. Instead of anger, there is love. Instead of bitterness, there is forgiveness. Instead of despair, there is hope.

> To them God chose to make known how great among the Gentiles are the riches of the glory of this mystery, which is Christ in you, the hope of glory. Colossians 1:27.

There is a mystery in following Jesus. Science, philosophy, and modernity would tell us that our faith is misplaced, that we are following a myth, that there is nothing beyond our senses. The mystery, that thing the non-believer seeks but can't find, is hope, and that hope is Christ in you. We live in freedom because we know that there is more than this life ahead. We are not shackled to sin, because Jesus set us free. We stand against the storm because we don't stand alone. That is our confidence, that we are not alone.

Tragedy is the great tester of the faith. When faced with troubling news or the loss of a loved one it is easy to feel alone, isolated, and helpless. But when we realize that the presence of Christ dwells inside of us, there is nothing that can strike us down.

When my nephew died I flew to Florida to give comfort to my brother. The constant question was, why? He was on drugs and ran into a busy street. The real question was, "why didn't God stop him?" They are not believers, so their questions would always end in despair. They have no hope, nothing to hold on to, but for the Christian, Jesus changes everything, and sorrow turns to dancing.

Jesus also said that we are to love our enemies and do good to those who persecute us. How is that possible? How can fallible people do the extraordinary? It is achievable because the ability does not lie in our own strength but in the strength of Christ in us.

When you come to realize that God has not left you alone, that he has given you the Spirit to fight for you, that the mystery hidden for thousand of years has been made known to you, when you realize all of this how can you not rejoice! Jesus changes everything!

Chapter 12
Believe In God

Jesus said, "Let not your hearts be troubled. Believe in God; believe also in me. In my Father's house are many rooms. If it were not so, would I have told you that I go to prepare a place for you? And if I go and prepare a place for you, I will come again and will take you to myself, that where I am you may be also" John 14:1-3.

Few of us live in secluded areas where there isn't any crime. Trouble surrounds us. School shootings, natural catastrophes, rape, murder, abortion, drug abuse; trouble is everywhere, if we want to take notice. It strikes fear at night, and it haunts our dreams; if we are involved.

Jesus steps onto the scene, a troubled time for the Israelites, and tells his disciples not to let their hearts be troubled. "In the world you will have trouble, but I have over come the world" (John 16:33). Easier said than done when you are faced with real problems, people trying to hurt you, or your family is explosive, few people will even talk to you, or your friends have

packed up and moved away. But the remedy to the trouble is not advice or counseling, but God himself. The catalyst for healing is our faith in Jesus, and a promise of hope.

The answer is a place in God's presence, and the promise of a room in his house. Can you imagine being invited to the White House for dinner? All the fancy table wear, a full staff to serve you, and the special clothes. I would be dumb struck. The honor and privilege to be in the president's home. But, what if at dinner he stood up and called you by name. "Andrew, I'm aware of your hard life, but I want you to know that I have prepared a room for you next to my son's. You are part of the family." It would be unbelievable.

This is exactly what God has promised us. He has prepared a room next to His Son's. We have nothing to worry about, ever again. The book of Revelation says, "Blessed are those who are invited to the marriage supper of the Lamb" (Revelation 19:9). Are you blessed? Do you belong to the family of God? If you do, you have no more troubles, because your future is secure. If you don't, all you need to do is trust in Jesus' act of love and power.

The promise, however, is future. Until he returns, or calls us home, we are responsible for living out our faith in such away that people see our good works and give glory to God. Our

purpose is to see new believers become fully devoted followers of Jesus, who in turn Disciple others. Why? Because we know the future, and the outcome of a troubled world. Therefore, we watch for his return, but keep focused on the work he has called us to do, even though it seems so long. It has been over 2000 years already. But be encouraged, the Apostle Peter wrote,

> But do not overlook this one fact, beloved, that with the Lord one day is as a thousand years, and a thousand years as one day. The Lord is not slow to fulfill his promise as some count slowness, but is patient toward you, not wishing that any should perish, but that all should reach repentance. 2 Peter 3:8,9.

I love this verse because it puts things into proper perspective. We look at life from our own vantage point, while God looks at it from an eternal perspective. Time is of no consequence to Him, whether one day or a thousand. But, there is a reason for his tardiness. It is for the sake of the perishing. There are still people who will come to faith, so we need to be patient. Peter continues

But the day of the Lord will come like a thief, and then the heavens will pass away with a roar, and the heavenly bodies will be burned up and dissolved, and the earth and the works that are done on it will be exposed. Since all these things are thus to be dissolved, what sort of people ought you to be in lives of holiness and godliness, waiting for and hastening the coming of the day of God, because of which the heavens will be set on fire and dissolved, and the heavenly bodies will melt as they burn! But according to his promise we are waiting for new heavens and a new earth in which righteousness dwells. 2 Peter3:10-13.

In order for our future home to be realized, Jesus has to return and bring judgment on those who have not believed. In order to make room for our new home he will destroy this creation. It will be judged and cleansed with fire. The result will be a new heaven and earth, one where sin and death no longer exist. But there is a caveat. We need to reach out to people now and live lives of holiness and godliness.

Living faithful lives for God now is the price we pay for a beautiful heavenly home in the future. So, what does living a holy life in a troubled world look like? It's about good character, trust,

and faith. It's about loving your neighbors, doing good to those who persecute you, and forgiving just as God, in Christ forgave us.

We are also called to live in community, which in our culture, especially the church, isn't as easy as we think. Most churches call themselves a community, but after their Sunday morning activities they scamper home and huddle around their own activities. Living in community is much bigger than we can ever imagine. The rewards are great if we are able to live and persevere through the hard times.

Troubles come and go, but God is eternal. We may face trouble or we may live a life free of the world's care. Either way we have this great promise of living with the Father. Through the strength of the Holy Spirit we can remain faithful every day.

There are days that I begin to lose heart. The weight of ministry, the difficulties of keeping a body of believers together, feels heavy on my shoulders. It would be easy to give up, to walk away and live like the world. But God has called me to something greater. I am part of His plan to disciple people. He has given me everything spiritual blessing that I need for today. And He has given a promise to live in his house in the future. All because of

67

what Jesus did. Now if that doesn't change everything, I don't know what does.

Chapter 13
On The Way

Jesus said, "Behold, I am coming soon, bringing my recompense with me, to repay each one for what he has done. I am the Alpha and the Omega, the first and the last, the beginning and the end" (Revelation 22:12,13).

Three times in the book of Revelation the phrase Alpha and Omega is used. The third time, quoted above, is a statement by Jesus. It is proceeded by a promise to return and a promise to judge people for their actions. The first time is quoted below and is attributed God. It too is proceeded by a promise of Jesus' return and an explanation that the whole world will see him and wail, presumably out of remorse, for crucifying him.

Behold, he is coming with the clouds, and every eye will see him, even those who pierced him, and all tribes of the earth will wail on account of him. Even so. Amen. "I am the Alpha and the Omega," says the Lord God, "who is

and who was and who is to come, the Almighty.

Revelation 1:7,8

The second time it is used it is spoken by the one sitting on the throne who promises to make all things new, give water to the thirsty and to judge the unrepentant.

> And he who was seated on the throne said, "Behold, I am making all things new." Also, he said, "Write this down, for these words are trustworthy and true." And he said to me, "It is done! I am the Alpha and the Omega, the beginning and the end. To the thirsty I will give from the spring of the water of life without payment. The one who conquers will have this heritage, and I will be his God and he will be my son. But as for the cowardly, the faithless, the detestable, as for murderers, the sexually immoral, sorcerers, idolaters, and all liars, their portion will be in the lake that burns with fire and sulfur, which is the second death. Revelation 21:5-8.

The phrase indicates the nature and ability of the one described. The beginning and end, the first and last are references

to the eternality of God. In the context, it is a statement of Jesus' divinity. He is the almighty God who has both the authority and ability to bring blessing and judgment. To those who have by faith given their lives to following Jesus, he gives life. To those who have rejected the gift of salvation he brings retribution and condemnation.

At times, when things are going well, it is easy to forget that our blessings come from the Father. But when times are tough, when we wonder if life is worth living, we cling to the promises of God's coming. We long for the new earth where every tear will be wiped away and all injustice will be redeemed. In those moments, it is natural for us to think of heavenly things.

Yet, the kingdom of God is at hand. Through the indwelling Spirit we live out the reality of the Kingdom everyday. We enjoy life because we know its true meaning. We live for God's glory in everything that we do, and reap the reward of seeing his love manifest through us to other people in hopes that they too will follow Jesus. There is great joy when we experience the reality of the kingdom on earth.

We shouldn't, however, forget our purpose and mission. Jesus is the Alpha and Omega and brings judgment on the unrighteous. If not for His patience fewer people will enter the

kingdom of God. If we forget our purpose we will waste our time, lose sight of the opportunities around us, and the condemnation of the unsaved will be the result of our complacency. When the time comes for the alpha and omega to be revealed in his glory, will we be found faithful?

The writer of Hebrews said, "it is appointed unto men once to die and then the judgement" (Hebrews 9:27). We will all stand before the judgement seat of Christ and be held accountable for our lives. Those who have been redeemed will be ushered into their reward, but those who have not been redeemed will be cast out into the second death. Where the torment of the soul is eternal.

Objections are often raised concerning the cruelty of God and the barbaric nature of an eternal death. Of course, there isn't a complaint about eternal life. The idea of eternal death can be repulsive. Yet, for many, the repulsive nature of stern damnation doesn't motivate them to share the gospel. They would rather picket God's actions than warn others about the consequences and offer them an alternative.

I am little better. Am I willing to step out of my comfort zone to see others come to know Jesus? How often to do I pass up opportunities to share the gospel because I don't feel like it, it's inconvenient, or because I am turned off by the individual? The

Apostle Paul said, "Note then the kindness and the severity of God: severity toward those who have fallen, but God's kindness to you, provided you continue in his kindness" (Romans 11:22). We don't question his kindness, so we shouldn't question his severity. It should, however, motivate us to preach the good news, "Therefore, knowing the fear of the Lord, we persuade others" (2 Corinthians 5:11).

There is comfort and concern in knowing the Alpha and the Omega. Comfort to those who have received salvation through their faith in the gospel of Christ. Concern for those who have rejected that faith and fall under God's wrath and condemnation. Their destiny is the fires of hell.

Where is your destiny? Does it lie in the promise of God's compassion and grace, or in God's promise of judgment and wrath? Everyone faces moments in their life where they must make a choice between the way of life or the way of darkness. If you are reading this and have never accepted God's gift of salvation this is your moment of decision. All you have to do is confess that you are a sinner, that you have rebelled against God's will, and that you believe that Jesus died for your sins and rose again to the glory of God. Then the adventure begins! I'm telling you, Jesus changes everything.

73

Chapter 14
Here Comes The Bride

The Spirit and the Bride say, "Come." And let the one who
hears say, "Come." And let the one who is thirsty
come…He who testifies to these things says, "Surely I am
coming soon." Amen. Come, Lord Jesus! (Revelation
22:17,20).

I enjoy my life. There are problems for sure, but nothing
that would have me on my knees begging Jesus to come today. I
know there are places in the world where that isn't so. There are
some who believe that the United States is on the cusp of the same
type of persecution. It seems to always be that way.

As I grow older it becomes more apparent that the reality
of Jesus' return is preferable than this life, growing old is God's
way of weaning us of this life; it's so true. It is with this
perspective that our older generation can give us encouragement.
Youth are bold and daring, until they settle down with a family.
Family life is all consuming, until you reach middle age and the
kids leave home. Our senior years are reflective about legacies

and grandchildren. And finally, our eyes will close and we will stand in the presence of our savior. That's life in a nutshell.

Whatever Lifestage you are in, my advice, enjoy it. Take life by the horns and seize the day! Love the Lord! Love others! Love your family! And smile, Jesus is coming soon. This changes everything!